CW00704913

The Sun, the M.

Dipo Baruwa-Etti is a playwright, poet, and filmmaker. In 2020, he was shortlisted for the George Devine Award and was the Channel 4 playwright on attachment at the Almeida Theatre. Upcoming work includes *An unfinished man* (The Yard Theatre, London). For screen, he has recently completed *The Last Days*, a BFI/BBC-backed short film as writer-director, and has several original projects in development. His poetry has been published in *The Good Journal, Ink Sweat & Tears, Amaryllis*, and showcased nationwide as part of End Hunger UK's touring exhibition on food insecurity. *The Sun, the Moon, and the Stars* is his debut play.

DIPO BARUWA-ETTI

The Sun, the Moon, and the Stars

faber

First published in 2021
by Faber and Faber Limited
74–77 Great Russell Street
London WC1B 3DA

Typeset by Brighton Gray
Printed and bound in the UK by CPI Group (Ltd), Croydon CR0 4YY

All rights reserved
© Dipo Baruwa-Etti, 2021

Dipo Baruwa-Etti is hereby identified as author
of this work in accordance with Section 77 of the
Copyright, Designs and Patents Act 1988

All rights whatsoever in this work, amateur or professional,
are strictly reserved. Applications for permission for any use
whatsoever, including performance rights, must be made in
advance, prior to any such proposed use, to United Agents,
12–26 Lexington Street, London W1F 0LE (email info@unitedagents.co.uk).
No performance may be given unless a licence has first been obtained

No performance may be given unless a licence
has first been obtained

This book is sold subject to the condition that it shall not,
by way of trade or otherwise, be lent, resold, hired out
or otherwise circulated without the publisher's prior consent
in any form of binding or cover other than that in which
it is published and without a similar condition including
this condition being imposed on the subsequent purchaser

A CIP record for this book
is available from the British Library

978-0-571-36922-5

2 4 6 8 10 9 7 5 3 1

Acknowledgements

Thank you to God, Mum, all my family and those who've been part of this play's journey including:

Nadia Fall, Kibong Tanji
Peter McKintosh, Oli Fenwick, Tingying Dong
Isabella Odoffin, Dannielle Lecointe, Justina Kehinde
Sarah Lyndon, Eleanor Butcher, all at Stratford East

Katie-Ann McDonough, Indhu Rubasingham
Tricia Wey, Chiedza Rwodzi, Rachel Summers
Joan Iyiola, Polly Bennett, The Mono Box
Bridie Donaghy, Rose Cobbe, Florence Hyde
Hannah Campbell, Jennifer Bakst, Harry Mackrill
Rebekah Murrell, Liz Daramola, Dinah Wood
Faber & Faber, The Yard, and Kiln Theatre

The Sun, the Moon, and the Stars was first performed at Theatre Royal Stratford East, London, on 2 June 2021, with the following cast and creative team:

Femi Kibong Tanji

Director Nadia Fall
Designer Peter McKintosh
Lighting Designer Oliver Fenwick
Sound Designer Tingying Dong
Movement Director Dannielle 'Rhimes' Lecointe
Assistant Director Justina Kehinde
Casting Director Isabella Odoffin CDG

Characters

Femi
twenties, a Black woman

Setting
London
Now

THE SUN, THE MOON, AND THE STARS

Note

Femi performs the entire play.
It's all from her point of view.

Left aligned: Femi speaking.
Centred text: Other characters speaking.
Right aligned: Stage directions.

Blank line: Pause.

Whaddya do when ya see uh man
at thuh edge of your bed
at midnight?
Thass thuh dilemma that drowns me.

D'ya scream?
D'ya close ya eyes?
D'ya pretend ya dreamin?
Guess it depends on if ya recognise him;
an' I do.

Iss ma bruthah.

Seun.
Juss hangin there like air.
'Cept it can't be.
That ain't uh possibility.
It can't be.
Issa impossibility –
seein ghosts.

But he don't even look like one.

He's silent.

Gentle.

'S'if lookin for ma guidance,

since I wos numbuh one.

Thuh one who came out inta thuh world firss

ta check for any hurdles

before he followed.

Thuh Taiwo ta his Kehinde.

It wos only eight minutes, but

ever since then, he let me lead thuh way.

I started dancin, then he did.

I started athletics, then he did.

I started partyin, then he did.

Our parents always acted like we were magic,

cos even though Yoruba people are more likely

ta have twins

than any othuh group on thuh planet

there was thuh idea that twins cood be a treasure

or tragic.

We had that power.

An' it cood nevuh be predicted.

Maybe thass why our parents were so lovin.

They'd throw us separate birthday parties

when we got foolhardly around thuh age o' ten
an' demanded separate themes.
They dint even scream when I chased Seun
thru thuh passage an' he fell,
hit his tooth and it chipped,
but just sat down patiently ta tell me why
I've gotta be calmer.
They were thuh sweetest.
Thuh most longsufferin.
Those memories of em make me smile – even if jussa lil –
an' I'm grateful they ain't gotta be here now.

Is he here now?

He can't be.
I tell maself iss juss me
knowin thuh trial starts tomorrow
an' conjure ma hands ta hug ma eyes,
tell ma mind to get a grip
sing one, two, three –
like mum taught me wen seekin harmony –
an' I wait for it to dissipate
an' slip inta uh futile state.

I feel thuh room tip upside down
an' empty isself.
Then open ma eyes agen.
Ma room's empty
like thuh rest of thuh flat
like iss been for thuh lass nine months.
I feel thuh flowin
thuh rush o' tears comin
an' thuh dam boutta break
like a china plate
so I quickly grab ma phone
bell Tiffany, Shadiya, an' Lexi
an' find ma catharsis in thuh club.

I move an' groove
play aloof when approached
by men who think they're smooth.
I slide an' wine an' suddenly
thuh music changes.
Missy Elliott plays.
I try boppin but thuh bank that ma mind is
collapses like iss 2008.
Cos we used ta dance ta this.

I rush ta thuh bathroom, but thuh girls are
so inta thuh vibe that they don't notice.
I wipe thuh sweat off ma face,
look in thuh mirror
an' see him in thuh reflection.
Hangin there agen.
Unlike an hour ago,
I know he's there.
Iss him.
Seun.

'What you doin?'
I ask, mad
cos all I want right now is
ta feel thuh bricks rise an'
thuh breeze go through thuh fabric of ma shirt
an' thuh braids un-plait themselves
an' ma belt unbuckle isself
but his presence has me walkin down
on uh upward movin escalator.
Iss like fallin off uh cliff
fallin in thuh sea
an' God knows I don't swim
so I juss struggle ta breathe.

I try to zoom outta thuh room
but he blocks thuh door.
'Whaddya want?'
I close ma eyes
sing one, two, three
but he juss throws hisself on me
an' takes me ta thuh past.

Thuh sun is down,
thuh sound o' thuh tide can be heard
swishin against thuh Margate sands.
Seun an' Lexi are dressed up,
his hand round her waist.
They're laughin, jokin
wen suddenly stentorian screams abound
louder than thuh crashin waves.
I try ta cover ma eyes, but can't.
I'm forced ta watch.

I vomit on thuh bathroom floor,
pulled back inta thuh now.
Seun stares at me sorrowfully.
I reach out for his hand,
but he flinches.

He's tense,

hangin there like he duz.

This don't make no sense so

I race outta thuh bathroom

an' see Tiff, Diya, an' Lexi dancin.

I wanna join em agen

but thuh flight's turbulence

an' thuh haziness are too much,

so I – I leave.

I get home, climb inta bed

get an F in sleep

Seun's weepin on repeat.

I think bout those men.

They stripped him of his crown

so effortlessly.

Treated his charcoal skin like concrete

when he wos cryin out in need.

I think bout Seun starin at me in that bathroom.

He dint speak but there wos pain in his eyes

tellin me so clearly wot he needs:

peace.

Mornin comes an' I get ready ta trek
from North Woolwich ta court.
On thuh bus, Tiff keeps pattin hur new weave
an' Diya's paintin nails
like they boutta go ta uh Burberry show,
but I can't stop thinkin bout
thuh fright of lass night.

We arrive at court,
where press lie out front.
They're like crocodiles,
cold-blooded an' cravin meat.
They waited unduh watuh
juss aftuh he died but now
creep out.
Their yellow eyes pokin about,
their teeth sharp ready ta bite
for clicks, hits, gains.
But not ta bring honour ta Seun's name.
If they wanted that,
they'd speak bout his talent.
How he wanted ta be an architect.

Design buildins that'd last generations.
Instead they juss talk bout his end
like he ain't uh real person.

We enter thuh gallery.
Tiff spots Lexi an' begins ta head t'wards her.
But I can't.
Thuh haziness starts ta return
an' ma chest gets heavy
as I see hur.
I dunno why, but I stop Tiff an' Diya goin there
an' declare that I wanna sit away.
                    'Why?'
Tiff asks, but I ignore her an' go elsewhere.
They follow, Lexi lookin baffled,
as thuh show begins.
Day one.
Openin statements.

Thuh prosecution start.
They talk lovin'ly bout Seun,
thuh words I fed em months ago
pour outta their mouths
an' spread across thuh room.

They talk bout mum an' dad,

thuh motorway madness

that mangled em an' made us

orphans at thirteen.

How Seun had been uh rock for me,

as we went from foster fam'ly ta fam'ly

till it could juss be him and me.

How he was uh great student,

determined ta live thuh life our parents

had back in Nigeria, but do it here.

Like they always dreamed of.

Till those men let their hate

infiltrate and took it all away.

Thass what our lawyer sez it was

but argues manslaughter

for uh 'more likely conviction'.

Bun dat.

We all know wot it wos.

Murder, cos they hated his skin.

Cos it wozza sin ta em that he was in their

part o' thuh country

with one of theirs.

But they're pleadin innocent

so we gotta sit thru this whole thin'.

Thuh prosecution finish
an' then iss thuh defence's turn.
Lies swarm in like bees
an' they all sting me.
Talkin bout self-defence,
how they nevah meant ta leave him dead,
wen they –
'OH MY GOD.
Why're they lettin you speak?
These are LIES!
They are GUILTY!'

Quickly, I'm silenced.
Quickly, I'm warned.
Quickly, I'm seen.
Seen as mad.

Thuh men are brought up
one by one
talk their trash
which is polished
an' sprinkled in gold.
If I'm bein really honest,

it sounds good

an' thuh conveniently broken CCTV

an' thuh mysterious lack of eye-witnesses

an' the police contaminatin thuh scene

surely helps their case.

But I know thuh jury will see.

Thuh media will see.

Or will they?

History ain't on our team.

History ain't thuh giver of peace.

Hisory ain't ever set us free.

Maybe iss gotta come from me.

On thuh train back home,

I think bout how imma get justice,

wen Tiff interrupts:

   'Why dint ya wanna sit with Lex, Femz?'

she asks.

   'You can't suddenly blame her for Seun's death,'

Diya adds.

I look at em

like they've juss asked me if I can pilot a plane

pushin their enquiries

ta thuh bottom o' thuh pile.

'We need to do sumthin.'

          'Bout Lexi? Yeah, I –'

Shadiya don't even finish thuh sentence, cos

she sees thuh fury in ma eyes

even thru thuh darkness of thuh underground.

Iss piercin ha heart an' she's boutta go inta cardiac arrest

but I keep starin, cos if I speak they'll say –

        'Femz, iss fine, what were you say'n?'

        'Femz?'

'I said, we need ta do sumthin.'

        'Bout what?'

'Bout these men.'

        'Whaddya mean?'

'They're gonna get away with it.'

        'They won't.'

Even they don't believe that,

but I don't push it.

Iss clear that undahstandin evades em

like equality evades our environment

so I jump off at North Greenwich

juss before thuh doors shut.
Before their reflexes can wake
an' get in ma way.

I wait for thuh nexx train,
get ta Canning Town then sit on thuh 474,
till it reaches ma door –
lonely trailin behind
like a shadow.
I wish I could get a restrainin order,
but, alas.
It even holds me in bed
but iss nuthin
compared ta thuh chill I get
when ma fone vibrates
an' I see that Lexi's callin.
I ignore it
an' try ta sleep but I can't keep still
so take uh pill.

Thuh blackness comes
an' iss refreshin
but wiv it runs in thuh tragedy
that Seun showed me.

It replays like uh scratched record,

hoards thuh space in ma mind.

Seun, Lexi, walkin.

Thuh men jumpin him.

Crown, stripped.

Skin, concrete.

Thuh same thing,

except this time at half speed.

More torturous somehow,

but allows me ta see . . .

Lexi, obsolete.

Lexi.

Obsolete.

Not clawin nor fightin

not pullin nor punchin

like she told us.

Hur fable is false

an' thass why ma spirit felt repulsed upon seein hur.

She dint struggle tryna save him.

She stood there.

Still.

Mouth agape.

Burnin thuh cape

that came thru her parent's DNA.

I jolt awake,
she too muss pay.

*

Thuh nexx day, I make ma way ta court alone
not in thuh mood for Tiff or Diya.
Boutta minit away, I see Lexi
leanin agenst uh wall
in all black
head down
eyes closed
cigarette burnin.
'Lexi.'
She turns round, conjurin up uh smile.
                              'Femz –'
'Don't Femz me,'
I say, though thuh innocence she wears
is almost enough ta make me break,
see hur for who I thought she was.

'Why'd you lie ta me?'
                    'What you talkin bout?'
She asks, like I'm dumb.

Like thuh tsunami that hit
nine months ago
knocked me out an' made ma brain
go back ta thuh age o' one.
'Ya stood still an' saw em declaw ma brutha,
thuh supposed love o' ya life
an' did nuthin.'

                    'That ain't true, Femz,
                        I tried ta stop em.'
'Don't lie ta me, Lexi.'

                            'I –'

'Please, Lexi.
I know.
Ya jumped ta thuh side
wen their fists crashed inta his body.
Ya stood wiv ya hand ovuh ya mouth
as it all went south.
Juss on mute till they left
an' he was already . . .'
Her lips quiver,
watuh comes ta ha eyes like uh hose
juss opened up an' soaked ha face.
She embraces reality.
Thuh disgrace she is.

'I'm sorry,'

she sez

like those eight characters

two words

one sentence

are uh portal ta thuh past

uh time machine

like iss gonna change anythin.

'I wanted ta help, I did.

I wanted ta kick em

push em

stab em

burn em

kill em

but cooden move

cooden say uh thin'

cooden even breathe.

I juss froze and –'

'Ya know why ya froze?

Cos ya hated him.'

She gasps.

'I shooda known thass how it wos gonna be
wen I let ya entuh our lives.
Wen I made ya ma bess frend
an' let ya convince Seun
ya were gonna be his gal,
his ride or die.
But ya dint know wot that meant, did ya?
An' ya still don't now.
Ur juss uh lil white gal
who don't see thuh world like it really is.
Who thinks *she's* in danguh but
don't see thuh world thru our eyes.
Seun's eyes.

'Ya parents dint even want ya ta date
ma brutha.
I saw it in their dirty looks ta one anutha,
in their refusal ta eat wot he cooked
an' I think ya loved
makin em shook.'

                  'I loved Seun.'

'Don't say his name.'

               'I wish it wooda been me steada him.'

I push ha against uh wall
an' if I could shoot lasers outta ma eyes,
I'd carve an A inta hur head.
A for accomplice.
A for accessory.
A for abettor.
But I don't get long ta think bout that
cos suddenly Tiff 'n' Diya have their hands on me.
'What you doin?'
Tiff screams
but iss rhetorical.
She don't care bout ma answuh.
I know cos her an' Diya grab Lexi
shield her in their arms
an' rush away.
'TELL THUH TRUTH,'
I scream aftuh em.
'Tell thuh truth,'
as they fade inta thuh background,
make their way inta court.

Uh shiver runs down ma spine.
Seun appears, no longuh hangin there
but feet firmly planted on thuh ground

thuh side of his lips emanating disappointment.

Mirrorin mum;

how she used ta look

whenevuh she'd get uh call from school

say'n one uh us did sommink.

Usually me, but thass wot firstborns are meanta do.

Taiwos are ment ta hav thuh first taste of thuh world,

report back

allowin thuh Kehindes ta be more careful, reflective.

Thass thuh only reason I got in trouble instead o' Seun.

Research.

Still it wos always me gettin told off.

Right now, Seun's got that look.

I'd nevah seen it on his face.

Usually he mirrored dad – an anger bare subtle

you were nevuh sure whether he was boutta make uh joke

or tell ya ta stood down

get thuh wooden spoon out

an' beat u while ur tryna keep ur finger on thuh ground.

He had mum's silent sadness,

which tried to move inta thuh sun –

cos happiness is ideal – but nevah cood

when disappointment visited.

'What'd ya do that for?'

I jump

not havin heard new words

escape his lips in so long,

but it don't emanate euphoria.

His tone's all dad.

I wonder if they've been givin him tips

since reunitin.

Wonder if thuh inheritance has strengthened

since reunitin.

Wonder if they think o' me

since reunitin.

But I don't say uh word

cos when iss dad's tone, you don't.

You juss force tears

till God sprinkles pity over him

like pounded yam in boilin water.

'I dint show you all of that

for you ta get revenge!

What are you, The Bride?'

'Don't reference Tarantino.

You know I can't stand him.'

                'Then don't be dumb,'
he shouts back s'if I wazzen defendin his honour;
guardin it like thuh Royal regalia.
We snap back inta our old habits,
an' though I'm baffled right now
I'm also glad thuh fear I saw in his eyes
when he firss appeared
at ma bedside
is now hidin.
This is more like thuh Seun I know.
Thuh one I can go toe ta toe wiv.

'If it weren't ta make things right,
then why'd ya show me all that?'

He rolls his eyes.
Sighs.

             'I want Lexi ta have peace . . .'
Lexi?

            'Ya saw how she froze like ice.
         I don't want that blockin her life.
           She needs ta move on.'

Thuh seed of offence
settles in soil an' starts germinatin wivin me.
Lexi sees thuh sun,
I'm thuh one that has thuh moon shadowin ovah ma life.
Thuh moon.
Always thuh moon.
Thass what I wanna say,
or ask why he don't juss go ta hur,
but before I can,
he's disappeared.
It don't matter anyway,

I nevah lissen ta him.

I rush inta court
juss as Lexi's called ta thuh stand
an' they ask hur what happend that night.

I look at hur,
she looks at me

an' she confesses that
she dint try ta peel em away from Seun.

Dint attempt ta protect his Black body from pain.
Dint unleash her fury on thuh men.
She tells thuh truth.

Some peepl gasp
an' others whisper till they're silenced.

Thuh defence tryta put sunglasses ovuh their mouths
ta dim their shine –
  'If you didn't have the urge to fight, Miss Lloyd,
    like you initially said,
   then how could it have been as violent
     as you described?'
they ask wen iss their turn ta quession Lexi
discreditin ev'rythin else
she sed happened that night.

Damn.

In ma periphery, I see uh sly smirk.
I turn an' see an olduh couple,
follow their gaze an' it leads ta one of thuh men.
Thuh ring leaduh.
I ain't looked at em since thuh beginnin,
but now I see they think they're winnin.

Thass wen I realise,
these men gettin life wooden even be enuf
wen Seun wos denied that.
Lexi froze an' I'll never forgive that
but this is bout those men
who stripped him of his crown,
treated that charcoal skin like concrete.
Peace will only come
wen I make em come undone.

*

I spend thuh rest o' thuh day
starin at thuh parents,
ma bile buildin an' buildin.
Wen we're done,
I hav more anger than
watuh in thuh Nile.
Ma heart's pumpin bare fast.
I follow em ta Monument,
jump on thuh District Line.
I dunno where I'm goin,
juss know I need ta show em
ya don't mess with ma brutha

an' get away with it.
I keep ma eyes glued ta em
till they finally get out at
Dagenham East
an' walk ta their house.

I wanna rush aftuh em as they head inside
but ma heart's still movin mad
so I let it pass.
I inch closuh ta thuh door
then turn on ma heels for thuh wall.
I lean against it an' see they're watchin *EastEnders*.
I ain't watched it in years,
but I stand there till thuh episode ends
wishin someone would script this moment for me
cos I ain't got no clue what I'm s'posd ta do.
All I know is that I'm fumin.
I wanna scene on thuh scale of
You ain't my mother! Yes, I am!
so I swallow the thrill of it all
an' bang on thuh door.

Thuh lights in thuh sittin room
disappear.
'I know you're in there!'

Moments later, I hear thuh croaky voice of thuh mum
as she opens thuh door.
She's uh fragile lil thin',
hands shakin, kinda like me.

'Whaddya want?'

She recognises me, which saves uh introduction
that we neither need nor want.

'Ma son ain't here, is he?'
'Ya got any othuhs ur preppin ta murder us?'

'Ma son dint murder anyone. Don't you –'
I stop her right there
before I knock hur unconscious
an' cut hur open
ta get thuh naivety outta her organs.
I tell hur I gotta check there are no more sons.
She denies me, so I tryta get thru thuh door
worm ma way in, but she's swift like uh mouse
an' blocks ma path.
We stare at each othuh an' if looks could kill
it'd be a warzone
out here in thuh front garden
of numbuh 62

with iss hollyhocks an' crooked wooden gate.
They'd be blown ta pieces,
along wiv thuh grinnin gnome that says welcome ta me –
iss face understandin an' creepy simultaneously.

'Ya son had no right takin that life.'
She opens her mouth ta fight ma words,
but I push her aside an' rush inta thuh house.
Screams
curses
blast thru thuh air
like missiles
as she an' hur husban' shout at me ta leave
an' she sez she's callin thuh police.

'I know ur protectin em.
They in thuh shed or summink?'
Thuh dad tries ta grab ma arm
but I punch him in thuh gut,
tell him never ta touch me.
Tell him I won't let another die,
not by their hands,
an' I'll kill whoevah I have ta.

He scurries outta thuh room
knowin I'm tellin thuh truth.
That ma fury could birth summink
wilder than uh wildfire.
So he scampers an' I scan round,
lookin for somethin' ta grip onto
when his mum returns
lookin prouda herself.

                    'I've called the police.'
Her hands are still shakin.
She looks like she's been cryin.
Normally, tears cause me to liquefy,
but tonight I'm solid,
harder than ever.
Thuh woe issa gift
so I juss give hur a round o' applause.
'How does it feel ta have birthed Satan hisself?'
Her mouth opens an' I swear
her gasp cooda been heard from Timbuktu.
She storms up ta me, fury as she defends her legacy.

                    'Ma son is an angel.
                    Would never harm uh fly.
                    Would never kill uh man.
                    I dint raise him that way.'

I feel thuh naivety – an hur spit –
fallin on me like debris
but I shake it off
an' I shake her off.

Well, I do a lil more than shake.

I push hur ta thuh ground.
Her frail lil body.
I kick her stomach like issa ball.
I shout,
scream.
'What d'ya mean?
I saw it with ma own two eyes.
An' ur son is sick.
Uh sick sick sick sick sick thing.
Not man,
but thing.
An' I juss wanna give advance warnin
that I will trample on him wen
he walks outta that place uh free man.
An' I will trample on you
an' ur husband
cos he's thuh product of both o' u.

Of ur parents.

An' their parents.

An' their parents.

An' their parents.

An' their parents.

An' their parents.

An' I won't be glad till u –

thuh begetters of thuh drunkard

thuh deviant

thuh denier –

suffer.

So if I were ya, I'd enjoy ma lass days of freedom.'

I turn round an' see hur husband juss standin by thuh door

an' know thass gonna cause an argument later.

I laugh ta myself as I head out,

heart pumpin,

beatin like it ain't since that day nine months ago.

Iss like I was growin this wrath in ma womb

an' finally gave birth.

But that was child one

an' I'm expectin triplets.

Now's not thuh time, though.

I hear thuh pigs oinkin – no siren – an' leg it.

I take uh pause after a few minutes
an' of course, Seun appears.
'I don't wanna hear it.'
                    'I dint say nuthin.'
'Good.'

                    'You wanna get some ice-cream?'
I roll ma eyes,
shake ma head.
Ice-cream?
Really?
I'm tryna get justice,
an' he's tryna get ice-cream
like he can even eat it.
                    'How bout karaoke?'
'Whaddya think this is?'
                    'Ya gonna get yaself in trouble
                    if you don't calm down for uh bit.'
'I ain't got time for that.'
                    'Not even karaoke?'
he asks wiv uh smile
hopin thuh curve will reel me in
knowin iss ma fav'rit thing ta do.

Was.

'Seun, no.

We need just –'

He starts ta sing.

I wanna scream at him

tell him ta stop, but

in spite of maself

I start ta melt.

I wanna join in –

his melody takin me back

ta sum o' thuh bess nights of our lives.

I don't sing back though.

He might look an' sound thuh exact same

but he's uh ghost.

So I push him out thuh way,

puttin an' end ta this display.

               'C'mon, Femz, let's –'

'No, Seun,

STOP it, okay?

Ya keep doin thuh most,

but ur dead.

You're dead.'

*

I go ta work.
They've got shifts ta fill
an' ma managuh asks if I'm interested in uh double.
Course I ain't – issa supermarket –
but I can't quit,
got bills ta pay init,
so I go in.

I'm scannin people's things but can't focus,
wantin ta plan ma revenge instead.
Figure out how I'm gonna dead these men.
I'm scannin an' scannin an' scannin
but I can't even buss uh smile at customers
an' tell em ta have uh great day
even if thass all I wish for most o' dem these days.
Ma managuh can sense it,
takes me off thuh tills an' tells me ta
pop tags round thuh store.
I give hur uh screwface cos . . .
Don't she see?
I gotta greatuh destiny now.
Once upon uh time, I actually enjoyed that,

reminded me of bein a lil girl

with ma shop set.

Walkin round thuh store is wen I gotta see

mosta ma colleagues,

bantered wiv em.

But that wos then.

Now, ma real purpose is tryna burst thru

but is bein held down by this job.

I can't hav that though

so I storm out.

As I get ta thuh flat,

I see Tiff and Diya standin outside.

Uggggggh.

'What're you guys doin here?'

They look at each utha

like they're Venus an' Serena

like they're bare tight an' nevah used ta fight ovuh me.

I'm boutta snap when Patience slithers

off uh nearby tree branch

an' wraps isself round ma shoulduhs.

'Should we sit in thuh park?'

'No.'

　　　　'How bout uh walk by thuh ferry?'

'Juss tell me why ya here.'

　　　　　'Iss bout Lexi.'

One.

Tw— No. No. No.

I'm gonna explode if I don't teach these ladies uh lesson

in courtesy right bout now

so I open ma mouth, but Tiffany interrupts.

　　　　　'She's in hospital.

　　　　　She tried ta kill herself.'

I pause.

Takin it in,

cos thass serious, ain't it?

Suicide.

'She tried ta kill haself?

Shame she dint succeed.'

They gasp an' I nod.

They ask me how I can say such uh thin'

an' thass when I get all Ice Queen on em.

'Tiffany. Shadiya.

Don't.

Juss don't.

You wanna gasp?

Gasp at ya lack of self-awareness.

Gasp at ya ignorance.

Gasp at ya inability ta read uh room.

I know they say don't judge uh book by iss cover

but when it comes ta mine, please do.

When I put on thuh I-don't-give-a-damn mask,

iss real.'

'Ya don't mean this, Femz.'

'Maybe ya right.

Maybe I shood go.'

They smile.

'I could help Lexi out.

I mean she wants ta die, right?

I could end it for ha.'

They cut their eyes at me,

tell me I've become so savage

an' they want nuthin ta do wiv me

if I'm gonna act this way,

before turnin away an' leavin me.

I get ma keys out an' find maself shakin.

Even though I've had bare arguments before today,

still, I'm shakin in complete disarray.

wen I feel him appear behind me

like uh gust o' wind.

          'Femz.'

Ugggggh.

          'Can ya go see her?'

he asks, s'if he dint juss hear wot I said.

          'She's been ya girl from day, Femz.'

he sez, s'if I don't know ma own history.

But they can't be uh part of whass ta come.

None of em.

Their fingerprints can't be on thuh ton

of bricks thass gonna rain down.

I've gotta wash ma hands, let em be gone

from me

wiv no temptation ta return.

Where I'm goin, I've gotta be on ma ones.

I don't say this ta Seun.

He shood know.

But, alas, he persists.

'Please, Femz.'

'Please wot, Seun?

Visit ur princess?

Thass all ya keep talkin bout.

Ya ain't once asked me how I am.

How I'm managin ta rise up.

How I ain't juss layin in bed for days,

weeks on end,

cos I did that too.

I dint leave ma bed for uh month

'cept for wen thuh girls dragged me

ta bury ya.

Then I continued in ma misery

wantin ta walk ta Waterloo Bridge

an' jump inta thuh Thames.

But ya don't even care bout me

or thuh moon shadowin ma life.

Thuh strife thass embedded isself

in ma bein.

Ya don't care bout me seein thuh sun,

but I ain't even sure thass so important right now

wen I know there's othuh people

all ovuh this city

standin on bridges, quessionin if they shood . . .

'Ghosts don't juss exist aftuh death.

I pass so many ev'ry single day

an' see thuh trauma in their eyes.

Thuh trauma of thuh ones leff behind.

Wonderin how they're gonna get by.

Frowin cos tragedy keeps drownin us.

Thus, we need ta do summink.

Me an' u.

An' I can see that u know that

this is bigguh than us.

'I'm tryna get justice

so we don't keep strugglin ta rise up

each day

cos all we're expectin is pain.

This is ma terrain now that

u, mum an' dad hav gone.

I cood jump,

but I have no nexx of kin,

no one ta collect ma belongins

so I wanna make sumthin of this

eternal lump in ma throat

an' if ya can't help wiv that,

then why ya even here?'

He looks me in thuh eyes like I'm mad.

I look at him like he's denyin me deliverance.

Then he cries.

I dint know ghosts cood cry

but he duz.

'Femz,

ur gonna see thuh sun.

Thuh sun will shine,

an' u will smile.

Thuh moon will fade,

u'll be okay.'

He's manipulatin me.

He's skirted ovuh evrythin I sed

an' is tryna trick me inta doin wot *he* wants.

He nevah did that before.
Or maybe he did.
Maybe I juss erased thuh bad
side o' him, like uh sketch that
I needed ta make perfect
for it ta go up in thuh gallery.

I can't hav that, can I?

I stare at him.
Drums begin ta bang in ma ear,
alongside thuh stampin of feet.
I smell thuh sweat of thousands,
shouts resoundin
hearts poundin.
Songs an' screams.
Demands an' pleas.
I feel thuh church tellin spirits ta flee,
evokin that childhood memory
is all that gives me strength
ta tell thuh othuh half o' me ta leave.
Ta forbid him from comin back.

'GET THEE BEHIND ME.'

*

I grab uh knife an' stab inta thuh sofa.
It feels so good.
I do it ovuh an' ovuh
instead o' goin ta court
ta hear thuh defence plead their case
for innocence.

I picture thuh three men,
an' stab inta em,
sumthin' inside me brewin
bringin an excitement that means I don't care.
Ain't no fear left in me.
I hav no frends, no fam'ly.
Issa madness,
but sadness is gone.

Holes forms in thuh sofa
an' I rip em open further,
like imma peel their skin apart.
Thuh fluff from inside spills out –
like their intestines will –
hittin thuh ground.

I continue ta dig in,

this sensation hittin diff'rent.

I don't eat.

Don't sleep.

Time has no monopoly ovuh me.

I juss stab an' stab an' stab

till I'm ready ta come face ta face wiv thuh men.

Till I'm resilient.

Till I'm strong.

Till I'm uh killuh.

An' wiv perfect timin,

thuh lawyer calls me

ta say thuh verdict's in.

I think bout thuh jury

remember their twelve faces

an' wonduh if an avalanche of Truth

suffocated em.

If they cood surprise an' not be skewed by thuh

defence's lies

bout self-defence.

History ain't on our side,

right?

But wot if thass changed.
Wot if this is thuh switch?
Thuh signal?
Wot if they'll see this as wot it is
an' lock thuh men up.
I hope that don't happen,
that there ain't been uh change
ta thuh status quo juss yet
cos if they're jailed, I'll nevuh get
ma hands on those beasts.

I chain ma anxieties up an' get ready ta go.
I pick out new clothes,
add colour ta my dry palette,
includin sum killuh red lipstick.
I obviously can't take uh knife inta court
they wooden even allow ma afro comb,
an' I ain't gettin thrown in jail for possession.
Nuthin less than murder.
I'm ready.

*

Tiff an' Diya are there.

Lexi too, wrists bandaged.

Some of Seun's friends tag along.

We all sit togethuh as thuh men are found . . .

Guilty.

Wivout even knowin, thuh men

get their way.

They getta escape ma fate

an' also paint this as an accident.

This weren't manslaughter.

It wos murder.

Yet people smile.

It wos murder.

Yet they sing.

It wos murder.

Yet they swan

round like justice was served.

But one to twenty-four years,

wotevuh thuh sentence,

ain't justice.
An' I can't wait uh year
let alone more,
this feelin I have needs ta leave now.

So I jump up
fists clenched
eyes locked on thuh second man's parents
one o' em carryin uh kid –
their grandchild, who looks identical ta man two –
an' I realise I don't need uh knife
ta make thuh men feel ma pain
wen ma hands can do thuh deed.
Wen ma hands can delivuh thunduh an' fire
destroy wot anyone loves an' desires most:
their kid.

I storm up ta thuh fam'ly
thuh child
but then
he looks right at me
screws his face so effortlessly

an' I freeze.

This overpowers me.
I ain't got wot those men do in their blood.

I rush out
inta thuh bathroom
body shakin
vision blurrin
but thuh mirror
reflects no tears.
Instead thuh black o' that night
once agen plays on repeat.

Seun an' Lexi sit in uh booth havin' a pub dinner,
laughin, chillin, flirtin
wen uh man is in front of em.

       'What're ya doin wiv him?'
Lexi rolls her eyes, don't reply
an' he skulks away
back ta his two frends.
Seun an' Lexi finish eatin
avoid watchin thuh men watchin em
an' make for thuh door.

       'Why's uh monkey wiv uh princess?'

Seun stops, then shakes his head
takes hold of Lexi's hand
so it don't go flyin ta thuh man's face
an' they leave – walk straight outside,
where there's uh moment of relief.

He wraps his arm round her waist.
Thanks God he dint hav ta beef tonight.
It wooda ruined their anniversary
an' he juss wants ta spend it peacefully.
They laugh bout thuh men
how they're so pathetic.
Laugh an' laugh.
                              'Oi, monkey!'
They turn ta find thuh firss man –
whose parents I thought I wood kill –
right behind em.
His fist collides wiv Seun's chest
an' he's uh hundred pounds heavier
an' eight inches talluh than ma brutha,
an wiv intent on his side
iss forceful enough for Seun
ta fall ta thuh floor.
Lexi jumps ta thuh side,

Seun tries ta get up, but his head
is given a kick
straight inta thuh concrete.
He opens his mouth ta speak,
but man two joins in
gives him a punch in thuh jaw,
zippin it shut.

'Seun,'
I scream, but ma voice can't be heard.
I try ta close ma eyes, but can't.
I'm forced ta re-watch
as Lexi stands there – still –
while Seun watches life drive by
at thuh speed of a snail.

I see him feel it all.
He feels each punch.
He feels each punch an' each kick.
He feels each kick an' thuh spit.
He feels thuh spit an' thuh belt used as uh whip.
He feels thuh whips an' his trousahs go down.
He feels his trousahs go down an' cries.
As they strip him.

Of his crown.

As they laugh.

Swear.

Spit.

He feels it all.

Thuh pee man three sprays on his body.

Thuh blood.

Thuh blood an' his tears.

Thuh tears an' thuh burns.

                    'Femi,'

he whispers

as thuh pain lingers.

I hadn't heard him call out for me before.

I tryta ignore space an' time:

'Seun?

SEUN?'

But he can't hear me

an' he can't cope

so he lets thuh hope go from

his beautiful brown skin.

His charcoal colour skin.

His smooth silky skin.

It weren't nevah ugly.
It weren't nevah ugly.
It weren't nevah ugly.
But they made it so.

I wake up on thuh bathroom floor
Tiff, Diya and Lexi kneelin beside me,
Lexi's bag spilt open on thuh ground
uh bottle of watuh in her hand.
They stare like I'm now tamed
Domesticated.
Can be trained.

                    'Femz, you alright?'
'No. Ma brutha's dead.'

They look ta one anothuh, then back at me.

                    'Femz, I . . .
        We're goin back ta mine. Gonna get sum Half
            Baked, watch uh film or two.
                    Please come.'

I don't wanna
but I don't say that.
Cos I'm tired.
I'm so damn tired.
So I nod
an' ask for uh moment alone.

I look in thuh mirror an' ma face is red.
Ha.
This Black gal's face is red.

I turn ta leave
when I see Lexi's makeup bag
sittin there.
Thuh one I told Seun ta get hur.
I pick it up an' look inside.

I look in thuh mirror
thinkin ta maself
bout how exhaustin this has been.
Uh rollercoaster ride.

But thuh tide ain't slowin
cos I still don't know whass nexx.

I still feel vex,
still feel thuh pain
still seek escape.
So I take out hur foundation
an' –

> *Femi takes out white foundation.*
> *She applies it to her face.*
> *She stares in the mirror.*

I wonduh if this'll bring thuh sun.
Peace.

'Seun?
Seun?

Is this thuh remedy?'

He dozzen come back,
so I leave,
hopin sumone will see me.
Or this version o' me.
Embrace me.

But they don't.

Lexi's busy talkin ta cameras now.

Tiff at hur right.

Diya at hur left.

Seun's face en masse in thuh air.

On t-shirts.

But not here.

I see thuh men's families talkin too.

Disappointed.

Thinkin bout appealin.

I dunno wot ta do,

I'm lost an' still searchin for thuh sun

then I wonduh

if Seun's appearance wozza message.

I wos thuh first born,

meant ta check out thuh world.

He wos thuh firss gone,

maybe he wos checkin out our afterlife.

Maybe his reappearance

wos tellin me that iss time

ta live thuh divine

with that fam'ly o' mine.

Time ta end it all.

I kick off thuh shoes that now feel like chains
an' walk,
feelin thuh grass
thuh stones
thuh earth.

I walk an' walk an' walk.
Ma feet bleed, but I don't care.

I walk an' walk an' walk.
Ma eyes want sleep, but I don't heed em.
Iss comin soon, be patient, I tell em
as I continue ta lead thuh way.

Darkness falls
an' I look around.
Realise I'm there.

Where he begged, on his knees.

I see thuh daffodils, lilies,
photos showin memories
teddy bears, notes filled wiv love

for ma dear brutha.

I see thuh sea.

I see thuh sand.

I see –

She wipes her face clean.

White doves fill every inch of thuh space.

Angels descend.

Violins play.

Uh gentle breeze swims in wiv ease.

Blossoms fall off thuh trees.

Pearls instead o' concrete.

I see –

'Seun.'

He smiles at me,

thuh kinda smile I ain't seen in uh while,

then whispers softly in ma ear.

Tells me not ta let it go.

Let wot go, I wanna say,

but he speeds away

flies towards thuh sky,

leavin me alone agen.

An' thass wen I see em.

For thuh firss time in ma life,

I see thuh stars.

Not juss one sun,

but stars

upon stars

upon stars.

I walked so far, am so far gone,

ta uh place where thuh stars come out.

An' I think on his words.

An' I look at thuh stars.

An' stretch out ma arms

wishin I was Elastigirl

an' keep reachin.

Reachin.

Reachin.

The End.